Renew Your Mind • Renew Your Heart • Hold onto God's Promises

~ By Patrice Sweeney

WestBow Press books may be ordered through booksellers or by contacting:

WestBow Press
A Division of Thomas Nelson & Zondervan
1663 Liberty Drive
Bloomington, IN 47403
www.westbowpress.com
1 (866) 928-1240

ISBN: 978-1-9736-4911-3 (sc)
ISBN: 978-1-9736-4912-0 (e)

Library of Congress Control Number: 2018914843

Print information available on the last page.

WestBow Press rev. date: 01/08/2019

COLOR✸Therapy

Renew Your Mind • Renew Your Heart • Hold onto God's Promises

Thank you
for picking up my
coloring book.

I hope and pray this
book blesses you
while renewing your
mind and heart
as you color and
meditate on God's word.

Patrice Sweeney

artist & designer
patrice_sweeney@yahoo.com
etsy.com/shop/ColorFunBooksCards

Give Thanks with a GRATEFUL Heart

Patrice Sweeney

1 Thessalonians 5:16-18 NIV
Rejoice always, pray continually,
give thanks in all circumstances; for this
is God's will for you in Christ Jesus.

1Corinthians 1:4 NIV

I always thank my God for you
because of his grace
given you in Christ Jesus.

~Patrice Sweeney

Let it Shine your LIGHT

Patrice Sweeney

Matthew 5:14-16 NLV

You are the light of the world. You cannot hide a city that is on a mountain.
Men do not light a lamp and put it under a basket. They put it on a table so it gives light to all in the house.
Let your light shine in front of men. Then they will see the good things you do and will honor your Father Who is in heaven.

Be Still and Know I Am God

Patrice Sweeney

Psalm 46:10 ESV

"Be still, and know that I am God.
I will be exalted
among the nations,
I will be exalted in the earth!"

Jeremiah 29:11 NIV

"For I know the plans I have for you,"
declares the LORD,
"plans to prosper you and not to harm you,
plans to give you hope and a future."

WAIT
ON THE LORD

Psalm 27:14 KJV
Wait on the LORD:
be of good courage,
and he shall strengthen
thine heart:
wait, I say,
on the LORD.

Patrice Sweeney

LET GO TRUST IN THE LORD

Patrice Sweeney

Proverbs 3:5-6 ESV

Trust in the LORD with all your heart,
and do not lean on your own understanding.
In all your ways acknowledge him,
and he will make straight your paths.

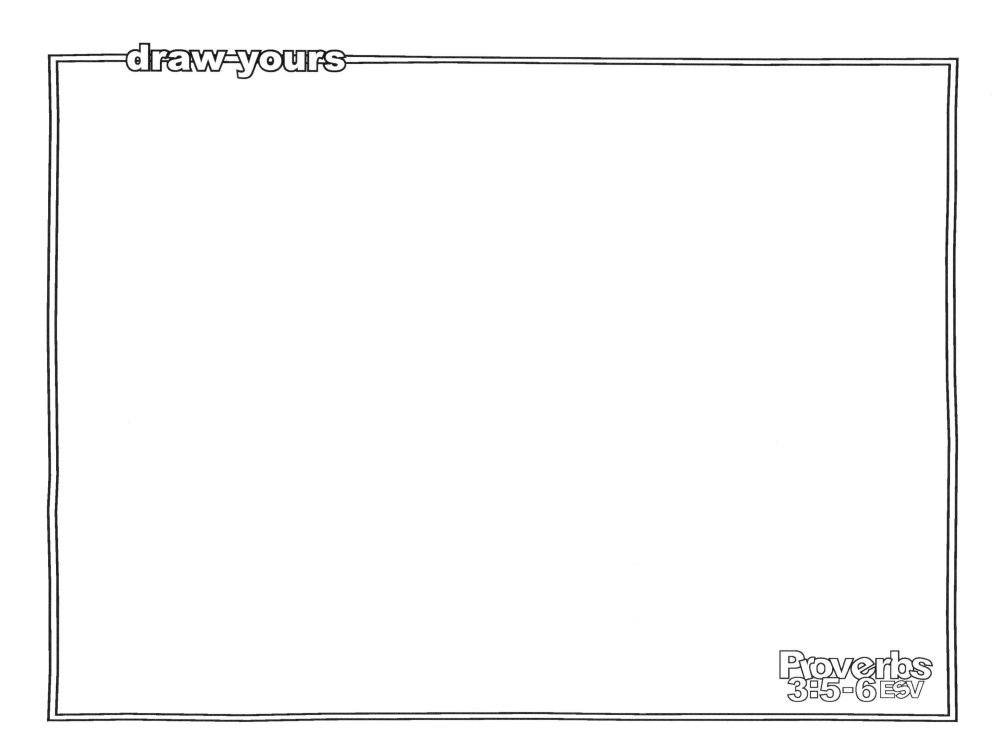

draw yours

Proverbs 3:5-6 ESV

Have COURAGE

Joshua
1:9 ESV

Have I not commanded you?
Be strong and courageous.
Do not be frightened, and do not be dismayed,
for the LORD your God is with you
wherever you go."

Patrice Sweeney

May the God of hope fill you with all joy and peace in believing, so that by the power of the Holy Spirit you may abound in hope.

God is

Faithful

Patrice Sweeney

Hebrews
10:23 NIV
Let us hold unswervingly to the hope we profess,
for he who promised is faithful.

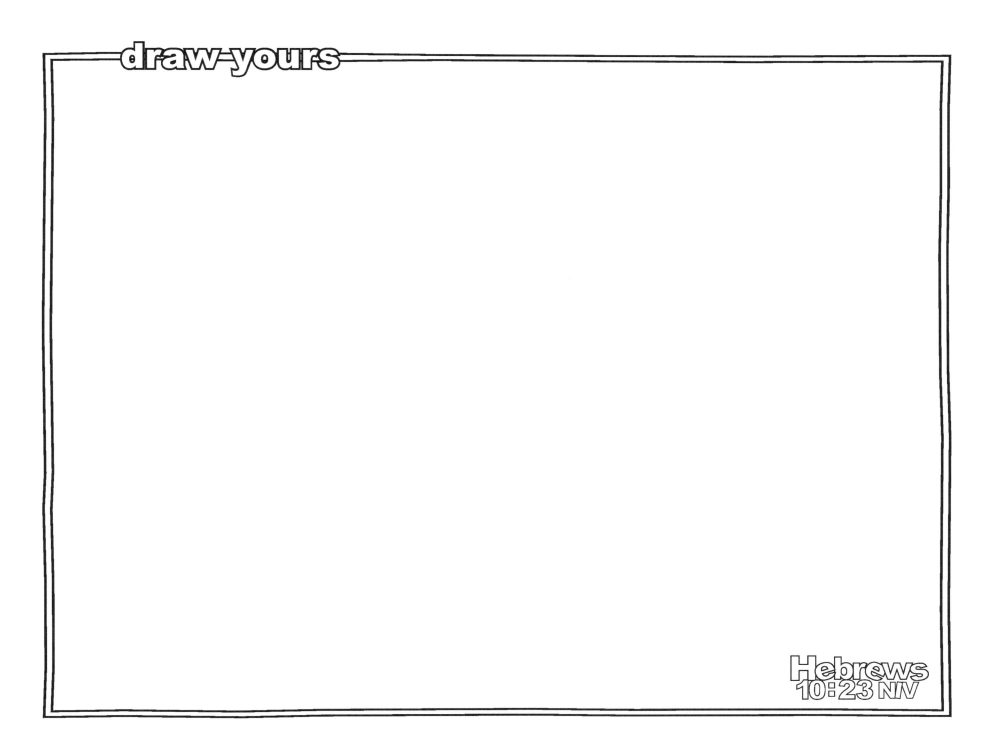

draw yours

Hebrews 10:23 NIV

Galatians 5:16-17 KJV

This I say then, Walk in the Spirit, and ye shall not fulfil the lust of the flesh.
For the flesh lusteth against the Spirit, and the Spirit against the flesh: and these are contrary
the one to the other: so that ye cannot do the things that ye would.

Psalm 105:4 NIV

Look to the LORD and his strength;
seek his face always.

SEEK HIS FACE ALWAYS

Patrice Sweeney

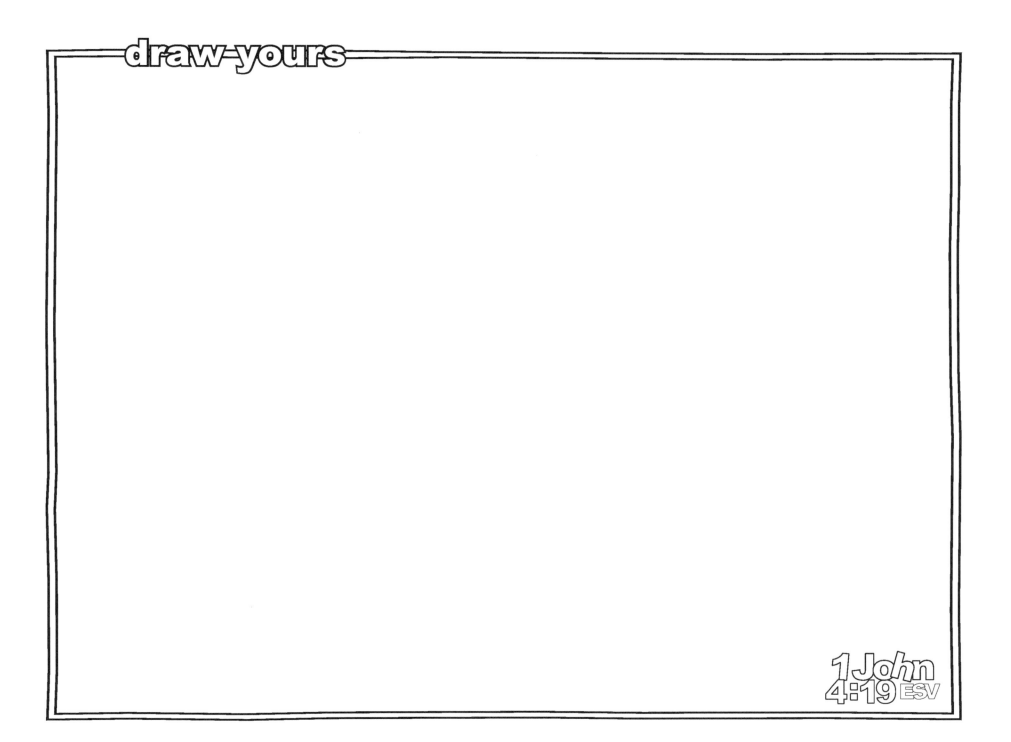

draw yours

1 John 4:19 ESV

Luke 10:27 ESV

" 'Love the Lord your God with all your heart and with all your soul and with all your strength and with all your mind' ; and, 'Love your neighbor as yourself.' "

LOVE

THE LORD WITH ALL YOUR HEART

Patrice Sweeney

FORgive THEM

Patrice Sweeney

Luke 23:34 NIV

Jesus said, "Father, forgive them,
for they do not know what they are doing."

Isaiah 9:6 ESV

For to us a child is born, to us a son is given;
and the government shall be upon his shoulder,
and his name shall be called
Wonderful Counselor, Mighty God,
Everlasting Father,
Prince of Peace.

PEACE

CAST ALL YOUR CARES ON HIM

Patrice Sweeney

Peter 5:7 KJV

Casting all your care upon him;
for he careth for you.

His Mercy Endures Forever

Patrice Sweeney

Psalm 118:1-4 KJV

O give thanks unto the Lord; for he is good: because his mercy endureth for ever. Let Israel now say,
that his mercy endureth for ever. Let the house of Aaron now say, that his mercy endureth for ever.
Let them now that fear the Lord say, that his mercy endureth for ever.

PATIENCE

Patrice Sweeney

Wait for the Lord

Psalm 27:14 KJV

Wait on the LORD:
be of good courage,
and he shall strengthen thine heart:
wait, I say, on the LORD.

FAITH
MAKES THINGS POSSIBLE

Patrice Sweeney

Luke 1:37 ESV
For nothing will be
impossible with God.

REST IN THE LORD

Patrice Sweeney

Psalm 62:5 NIV

Yes, my soul,
find rest in God;
my hope comes
from him.

♡ **1 Corinthians 13:4-8 NIV**

Love is patient, love is kind. It does not envy,
it does not boast, it is not proud.
It does not dishonor others,
it is not self-seeking, it is not easily angered,
it keeps no record of wrongs.
Love does not delight in evil
but rejoices with the truth. It always protects,
always trusts, always hopes, always perseveres.
Love never fails.
But where there are prophecies,
they will cease; where there are tongues,
they will be stilled; where there is knowledge,
it will pass away.

About The Book

Color Therapy places ageless Biblical Truth in the contemporary design of this hand-crafted coloring book. It is a tool designed to provide another way to meditate on God's Word and His promises. As you utilize the *Color Therapy* coloring book, you will find a deeper connection to God. In the quiet time of creativity and renewal, God's Word comes alive, facilitating healing in your heart, soul and mind. Reading the verses along with prayer, brings a response of clarity, as well as a feeling of renewal. There is power in the Word of God, and as we encounter each situation in life, the Holy Spirit gives renewed direction. Allow His Word to come alive, as you tap into your creativity as you color each page, and immerse yourself in each verse.